Helen

Happy Birthday 1985

With love

Pat

KAY GOULD-CASKEY

WITHIN THE BONES OF MEMORY

FALLING WATER PRESS • ANN ARBOR, MI • 1984

THANK YOU

Jim
Chosen to give beyond The All.
Who knows the breath of stones
and secrets of the heart.

Jess
Whose patience goes beyond
little girl years.
Whose dance is pure delight.

Raina
Weaver of starthreads. Gentle creature.
Life's knowing hand upon itself.

Jay
Who finds the struggling soul, and feeds
the hungry beast. Who helped by being a
part of the most difficult decision.

Dora
No mere taster of life, but one
who smacks her lips after every tasty
morsel.
Who teaches us all to enjoy the feast.
Thank you for your boundless generosity.

Karen
Romantic spirit. Twenty years—
a finer friend I could not ask.
Thank you for the listening.

Patricia	Who dances the dream and keeps it alive. Who reminds us we do not need candles to make a wish.
Connie	Who is not afraid to find life in the ashes. Thank you for sharing your home.
Louis	Quiet courage on the march. Courier of laughter. Thank you for friendship before and after life asked us to let go.
My Family	Thank you for love, giving, and the freedom to be.

Thank you, Keith Taylor and Christine Golus,
        for answering your phone
        and for the expert technical advice.

Thank you, Karl Pohrt, for sharing your knowledge
        and your time.

To Cas

Thrower of boomerangs into the night.
Silent traveller by my side.

The rock falls clean and straight into the water
more times than it used to.

Thank you.

CONTENTS

WITHIN THE BONES OF MEMORY

INTRODUCTION

What follows is a description, not a definition. I do not know how to define what lives between these covers, nor would I if I could. To name would be to limit. To name would be to claim knowledge I do not possess. I can, however, describe the process by which this book came about.

The words came through as more than words. I watched each scene within this book. I heard the words come through my lips. I felt the bite of winter, cold and sharp, smelled smoke and forest pine. When Blowing Grass spoke of sorrow, it was my sorrow. His joy, his quiet, his touch, were as my own.

This book is a selection from a series of events that has often happened over the last three years when I sat, eyes closed, my hands upon my husband's head while he rested it in my lap. Sometimes I watched Blowing Grass as one would watch his movements in a movie, separate from me, third person. This happened in many scenes, such as "The Cutting Line," "The Marshes," and "Stone of the Moon." However, I not only witnessed his movements, I also knew his thoughts, his feelings.

Other times he was not separate from me. When I looked at his hands, holding the pod and the rusted nail, they were my hands. The pain in "Sacred Water" shot through my leg as I said the words. Whenever Blowing Grass spoke directly, I spoke the actual words, not description of them. I felt them flow as any conversation flows.

When I sit with people other than my husband, holding their head or hands, Blowing Grass does not come through. Instead, each time it is someone else. It is especially interesting to me that with every person the words change in style and content. And always they speak in metaphor about something going on in that person's life.

What I have experienced may be no more than a variation on the way words come to writers, or it may be something else. I do not know.

THE CUTTING LINE

A wooden post stands dark in snow. Shadow of a single wire stretches beyond the line of sky, binding post to post. Blowing Grass stands, hand stopping on the new cut wood. Question becomes his thought. Why does this line that cuts sleeping prairies slice his heart and halt his breath?

He walks the shadow line, following until the sun warms his other shoulder. It is a line of no direction, but enclosure. The wire, cold between his fingers, brings a sadness. Rawhide and wood carry memory of life. This brittle strand has never held life's seed, and makes him tremble as he feels its containment.

SPIDERWEB

By full moonlight he sits and watches a spider spin her web. She moves quickly, without hesitation, her determination revealed. Movements appear to be random and with no design, but as the moon rises in the sky, pattern develops.

He is seated upon the ground. There was a rainfall earlier in the day and the grass is wet. Rain-scent fills him. Some of his favorite moments are after the storm passes and before all evidence of its presence fades.

The night breeze blows a damp leaf against his skin. It feels cool and a part of him. He is careful not to disturb the moisture held by the leaves and grass. Night sounds greet his ears. He recognizes them from his boyhood when the Old One would teach him to listen and hear. He not only recognizes the source, but also its direction and distance. Placing the origin of the sounds around him, he knows better where he breathes and moves.

Again his eyes seek the spider. She works as if he is not there. Whether she senses his presence and knows he will not harm, or whether she does not notice him, he knows not. She is busy connecting one leaf to another, one twig to another, weaving a tapestry between them.

He thinks about the things that his mother has woven. He remembers as a boy watching the women weaving baskets and blankets in the camp; a quiet activity, a noble one. And as he watched the women he began to feel them weaving not only what they held between their hands, but also the life breathing within their hearts. It was a weaving of families; knowing what parts to bind tightly, what parts to allow to flow— knowing how much tension to pull between threads, and how much grace to allow.

Eyes tracing the web, he begins to recognize times in his life along lines of the silk. He wonders where he is at that moment—where in the weaving of the dream he would be. Is he already there, or is he in the unwoven part, yet to be defined?

As the night builds, she shows no signs of tiring. The measured rhythm of the weaver's dance compels her. Watching, hour after hour, as the moon continues her journey across the horizon places life before him, and he begins to see the patterns more clearly, the spaces more sharply.

He has now located himself, not in the center, but between center and outer edge. He knows he would have found himself upon one of the major threads when the moon journeyed lower in the sky, but tonight he is in-between, floating, not seeking direction. Being in-between brings a giving-hand feeling.

He realizes life webs many choices around him. Yet, his path clearly leads in one direction. He has felt that direction warm his breath through many winters. He gives it no name. He gives it no sign. But he allows it room and a voice. When it speaks, he has learned to listen. His body and his mind grow silent, his soul attentive. The tension-fist of the great silk threads joins with the open-hand of those between.

The wind moves through the tapestry now, making it shimmer and dance in the moonlight. In times past he has gathered abandoned webs and carefully tucked them into the pouch he carries soft against his skin. He keeps them close to remind him of the structure of life, and all that moves within him.

This one he will leave. It is just beginning to serve its purpose. When geese fly across the face of the moon, it will be time to carry it through the winter, safe in his special place.

WHEAT

H e holds a stem of wheat between his eyes and the sky. Light passes through the fibers, filling them with the sun's life, the sun's color. Moving his fingers along the shaft and over the kernels, the unity, the closeness, touches his heart; each seed in a space just large enough for it to grow as it must—individually defined and complete. Yet, only together with the others will the seed know its power.

The women will grind it, and give it use. They will feed it into the fire and give it another name. And he will eat, and not forget its source.

THE TEACHER

Autumn sun. The earth is crisp. As a boy of nine winters he stoops upon a flat rock that overhangs the river. He breathes, and the brittle air fills him with life. He looks into the water, swift and clear. His eyes are seeking an old friend; a large fish who lives here by the rock.

Long months he has watched her growing, changing as the seasons change. He is doing as his grandfather taught him: becoming that which he hunts. He knows this fish he will never catch, will never try to catch. She is his teacher.

He slips his hand into the water, holding it silent. In time she comes, nudging his fingertips with her mouth, seeking something to eat.

Lying upon his belly, his face a whisper-breath from the water surface, he peers under the jutting edge into the shadows. She hangs, silver in the dark, resting from the heat of the sun. As he thinks about fish-catching, her movements flow through his body: the tautness, the silent breath, the flash of form.

He will return after the great snows have passed, and his movements will be swift and smooth, for he will have lived them many times.

He stands, back to the sun, shadow reaching across the river, touching the other side. He knows after the leaves of fire and sun fall and become part of the earth, she will come to the rock no more. And when the winter-stilled waters speak again, he will move as she has taught him.

GHOST OF DROUGHT

"The growing season has been long hot days of no rain. The earth dries up and blows away as I move my feet across her breast. Rivers that roared through my early boyhood now lie silent. Weariness draws the face of my people.

"A large dancing fire is built to ask for healing of the land. As the flames die in deepest night, and the fire bed cools to grey, we hope the summer also cools.

"The corn turned brown before it gave. The sisters and brothers of the field run where water still flows. Our hunters walk far and bring back little. Food gathering for winter does not stop with fading light. What lies ahead, shadowed in snow and silence, remains unspoken. Fear grips with eagle claws.

"After the fire circle breathes no smoke, women and children gather the ashes in large baskets, carry them to the fields and scatter the ghost of drought upon the wind. Next year the grasses will grow tall from the heat of this season.

"The fire is out; summer becomes memory. Winds of the falling leaf moon cool the burnt land.

"We wait for the grey bear of winter to walk through our camp. I want to be the first to see him as he approaches, swelling me with more importance than my three and ten winters. I wait outside the camp, but he does not pass by me.

"A small bird lands on a branch above my head, singing a song I do not know. It is the only time I will ever see the bird, or hear her song."

THE MARSHES

In the marshes the grasses nod and bow above him. It is the season he comes to watch and wait as the ducks fly in, skim the water, and settle. Hours dissolve around him as his insides fill with the birds. No landing mirrors another, his eyes catching the differences like sparks of light in an instant gone. He has not come as one who hunts, but as one who seeks; one who seeks with heart, and not with hands.

The coolness of the marsh lays upon the water, a gentle gift to the land. Even as the sun climbs to the center of the sky, she does not touch him. His insides fill with the sound of wings in flight and movement of landings that rib the water in their wake.

He wonders how it feels to be at home in the sky, to be at home upon the water, to glide from one to the other in a single breath of time. He admires the birds greatly. What they do naturally can only fill his dreams.

A mother with trailing young weaves her way through a forest of cattails and water grass. Many years later, while resting upon a hill, watching a train divide the land of flowing grasses, he will remember the row of little ones and how they crossed his eye, one by one. A cool peace will envelop him as his early days in the marshlands bathe the scene before him in gentle image.

Evening thickens as mist rises from the water. The shadow world awakens around him. Day birds have quieted and found their places as evening sounds pierce the night veils: voices from unseen singers. He and the invisible ones sit and share this night.

A piece of moon hangs in the sky, orange and muted, yet brilliant enough to glaze the ripples ringing the water grass. The face of the pond shimmers with her light.

STONE OF THE MOON

A dot of light rests in his palm, small moon from an unseen shore. Over and over he opens his hand, rolls the light between his fingers, and closes again.

It is a gift from a white man seeking passage through the land. The man told him of the big salty waters, and the small shelled creature that made the tiny stone-of-the-moon and carried it inside itself. It puzzles him; stone hard, yet grown inside a shell like a seed.

If it is a seed, it is too hard to grow and sprout life. Never has he seen a seed that from the beginning cannot become something else. Feeling it not to be a seed, he wonders why a creature would make a rock within itself.

Be it rock or seed or neither, he likes it and keeps it in his bundle. To know the name by which men call it holds no power.

THE POD

L eaves of changing colors spread above him, cutting the sky into pieces of blue. He rests against the trunk, feeling life flow from roots to sky and back again. His grandfather's grandfather knew this tree.

He picks up a pod that has fallen from a low-hanging branch. Soft and brown, it fits in his palm, as long as his hand is wide. He runs his fingers along its surface; crispness lies beneath the down. Hidden forms swell the pod into ripe fullness.

Slowly he coaxes it open, gently loosening the edges. The sun quickly slips in, revealing its contents. The inside shimmers soft and sun-gold; seeds dark, moist and quiet are joined to the spine.

He asks forgiveness for stopping their growth to satisfy his need to know. Silently, he folds the halves back together, makes a mark in the earth to cradle the pod, and with a gentle hand smooths the ground to cover it.

THE CHAIR

"There is much about the whites I do not understand.

"I once saw a white man riding a horse, something made of wood strapped behind him. I hid in the water grass; the fish I had been watching slipped away. Man and horse drank from the river while my eyes followed the lines of the wooden thing.

"Many years later I learned it was called a chair, and it stood on the ground to hold a sitting man. I touched the wood to know its strength. Slowly I lowered my body and sat as I had seen. Only my feet could touch the grass. I shifted from side to side trying to find the comfort I was told was there. The wood kept it hidden. Never had I felt so stiff, separated from the earth.

"I do not understand why a man would choose not to sit on the earth who breathes, soft with grass. And I have laughed many times remembering the man, the horse, and the chair. Did he carry it wherever he went to have a place to sit?"

SITTING IN THE FIELD

An old man, he sits, bundled in his robes, staring into the fire in his teepee. The flames reflect from his face as he sees a time past.

"When I was young and it was time to hunt, the men would be excited about what they would bring back to the camp. They were good hunters; there would be plenty to eat.

"I wanted to be alone. My feet walked best with no one's shadow beside them. I would not tell my legs where to walk, but listened to their direction. They told me much.

"One hunting day I walked to the place of dancing grasses which never stop moving in the prairie winds. Slowly I wove myself into the grass until I could see nothing else. I sat, a crooked trail leading to me from where I had come. I watched the wind make straight the grass I had bent. The path gone, only the earth and sky saw me there.

"My breathing and my heart became quiet. My skin no longer held me separate from the field. I sat, all signs of my coming gone. I felt rooted in the womb of the prairie.

"I would go back to camp that night, and many others, with hands empty. I did not return with an empty heart."

THE HUMMING BIRD

The tiny bird hovers, piercing the air: quick, crisp. Her wings blur, moving faster than anything he has known. As he watches, his eyes search beyond this rhythm for her feet. He can recall at will the feet of others: the hawk, the duck, long-toed walking birds. Those of the humming bird are easily forgotten.

Until this day he has only remembered her darting among the white and yellow flowers, as slippery in flight as the great silver fish swimming the river. From this moment he will also remember her feet and her times of rest, hidden from his eyes.

BIRCH IN SNOW

"I remember when the Old One lost his sight. It was as if the stars had been swallowed by the night. He said their lights still lived in his head, but not through his eyes.

"Walking beside him I tried to guide his feet upon the path. He smiled at my efforts as he made his way. He needed no one's eyes.

"That winter he taught me to see, for the first time, the birch in snow. I saw it with my hands and the side of my face. Its image burned into me as I explored with eyes covered, hidden from light.

"He slipped through the forest and I followed with steps unsure. I did not fear where he would lead, but that my feet would drag like stone and my legs crumble upon the ground like dried twigs.

"I kept walking, the back of his robe tight between my fingers. The moon in silence pulled the night across the sky. He made no sound as he drew me between the trees. I expected a twig, a branch, a hidden stone to catch his foot and announce our coming. Never did this happen. His steps became lighter while I crackled behind.

"The hawk's shadow slid over the fields as we rested on a large rock. Grandfather spoke of how shadows touch all in their path, leaving no mark, making no sound. He told me when I could hear the flight of shadows and the voice of the rock, my steps would know silence.

"We tracked the sun with the backs of our eyes, and by the patterns of warmth on our faces. Night brought the cool winds.

"My fingers saw. My feet saw. The tree up the back of me saw. I had grown beyond my skin.

"He knew the colors of birds by the sound of their wings; the colors of trees by the smell and touch of their bark. His fingers following the tracks along the trunk into the ground told him things he would never share.

"He knew spring by her songs and her whispers in the night. The wind revealed to him things I would never see. The scent of rain came to him before all others. He knew the winter's strength before the trees stood bare. But my favorite was the birch in snow— silence in white—moon soft across the fields—owl of snow calling in the dark.

"I know to be blind is not to be without sight. It can be the beginning of vision."

WINTER WALKER

"When I see Grandfather now, it is not with my eyes. It is the knowing of bones. He was called the Winter Walker, and walked the land most when the earth was white; the sound of his footsteps the same as falling snow.

"I remember sitting on the rock, the sky falling white around us. I touched Grandfather's face and read his life upon the lines, seeing his boyhood and the Old One who taught him to know the land. While we rested I could feel the Ancient One watching from the shadows.

"He was not our only companion in the short days of winter. As we walked, another walked with us. Laying my hand upon Grandfather's robe I could hear his grandmother singing.

"The robe had been her gift to him; a gift of warmth for a life of many winters. As the long days of sewing stretched behind her, the robe grew in beauty and weight, strengthened by her hands and blessed by her songs as the threads wove her voice into its heart.

"She had sewn feathers of the winter grouse on one shoulder and a small branch on the side over his heart. It was the first branch he had touched as his life began, and it would be with him as he stepped from life.

"Grandfather told me her songs helped his feet to move lightly over the land. Her voice would change as the landscape changed, warning when caution was needed. She could see all, and her voice knew no lies. His steps were clearer than when, a young man with sight, he walked these same hills.

"I knew he was not listening to the snapping of twigs underfoot, but was hearing the movement of the earth. He was listening to her as she sang him through the forest."

SACRED WATER

D eep to his knees in snow, he casts a briefer shadow upon the land. Many days of walking follow him. In his right hand he carries a staff with which he tests the drifts ahead.

The Old One told him he would walk these lands again. He remembers that first journey, in summer, with grass tall as the snow is now high. The images spreading before him are not the same. Seasons and time have changed the landscape.

At night in his camp he layers needles of pine between the leathers to soften winter's bite. He unbinds his injured knee to feel the air again. When all around him is frozen and silent, the pain reminds him that inside he is warm and alive.

With day the great birds soar above him. A healing sound surrounds him in this silent world as their wings cut the winter air. The sun rises, throwing their shadows before him, dancing their flight upon the earth.

He feels a tap on his shoulder. The Old One guides him, keeping his feet upon the path that sleeps beneath the snow.

Suddenly, the land drops away. Rising above him the waterfall stands frozen in silence. This is where he and the Old One stopped before. A single shadow paints the snow at his feet. The great birds no longer grace the sky, having remained behind a day ago.

He remembers his grandfather's words, and listens through the silence. From the mountain of ice he senses the movement of water deep within—water protected from winter's stilling hand by its own frozen breath. The Old One told him of the Sacred Water that time and the seasons could not touch. He lays a robe upon the ground and sits beside the crystal column.

As shadows grow longer he begins to feel the flow of Sacred Water within himself, echoing the sound and rhythm of his ancient companion. Together, they breathe beyond the measure of days.

CASTING OF SHADOWS

A dried twig stands straight in earth that has been smoothed. He sits watching the thin shadow move from line, to no line, to line again. His fingers trace the trail in the soft earth.

The journey of time, its pattern through life, speaks in question. Is the knowing of patterns the knowing of life? Does the marked land speak truth of the hidden depths? Do the lines cast by trees, grass, and people make him more aware of the movements shadows do not touch?

Time to the eye is the slow dance of sun, of moon, of stars. It is the sharp line of trees in snow, softened by the returning green.

How does the womb of earth know the passage of time? How does the core of his being know the changes of time? Do the bones of his father and grandfather know time?

When bone is strong and stands like the twig in the earth, there is a casting of shadows. When bone powders, joining the earth, there are no shadows.

HEART CIRCLES

The heart lays heavy; the soul does not move when the earth is not right. The insides of a man mourn for his mother in much the same way. Earth must be right or man cannot be right, for it is upon her breast that he suckles. But, unlike an infant, he is the caretaker of the earth. She who nourishes him, he must also nourish. The great circle that surrounds the earth cannot be complete until she breathes within his soul. The circle around a man's heart will not meet until this is so.

Many nights in front of the fire his father and the Old One shared gentle warmth of quiet words. They spoke of how things fall out when there are holes in the heart circle. While still a boy he searched for this image in his head. Now a man, he understands it is vision never to be seen, but to be known. It is known when he looks into a man's eyes because they reflect, as the moon, the source.

The long empty winter after fever took his wife rattles through the bones of memory. Pain ripped a hole so deep he thought his heart would fall from his body, as a singing bird, pierced by an arrow, falls silent from its nest.

Winter melted into spring, and night after night she came to him bringing threads from the moon, shining and clear. With fresh grasses he pulled from the earth, together they wove a new circle. Before her death, the circle had been of only grasses and roots.

He felt the light. It was good. And years later, when he married again, he knew that Threads-of-the-Moon Wife was helping hold the woman of earth safe in his heart.

THE JOURNEY

"The journey has begun. The direction is set. But just as the river carries the canoe, so you, too, must use your paddle to guide it, keep it from running aground, and splitting on rocks."

He speaks as he sits in his canoe, a time-lined face framed by blowing strands of white. Mist rises from the water, clouding his image. As the mist clears he has become transparent, and through that body stooped with age appears a younger man, sitting straight and tall.

He knows the big rapids lie ahead. The men in camp have talked many years about the point in the river where the water never rests. It is like the times in life when there is turmoil; the water froths and nothing is at peace. Part of the river is always this way. Other places, reflection is undisturbed, and the sky is as clear below as above.

"Rapids test the strength of the canoe and the cunning of the man who sits in it. The endurance of both, the quality and determination are challenged. Much stamina is needed, and unclouded thoughts. Men do not put their canoes into the water at the point of rapids. Places of difficult passage live further into the journey.

"As in life, there are signs to indicate what lies ahead if your senses are keen and your attention sharp. The sound, the feel of the water, the way hair lies on your body, change. The skin that covers you senses it, too. Deep inside, you know the unseen is there. The excitement and the fear join as one. And when you make it to the other side, the triumph shows in your face and in your stance to those who recognize the struggle. Those who have never been there will not notice.

"The river, where rock breaks the water, does not reflect the moon. She chooses to rest in quieter places. Reflection cannot be clear where there is no peace. Concentration is needed, not reflection. Reflection lives in yesterday and divides your thinking. Concentration keeps you in 'the time' as you pass through, allowing you full attention for the trail you mark this day. Eyes that look behind never guide the canoe.

"Nothing tarries here. The water rushes on her way; all she carries goes with her. Once the river passes beyond this place, it never returns. Think on this. It never returns. It is also never the same. But, unlike man, she shows no fractures. She exhibits no bruises and quickly flows together again. No anger is carried—no bitterness. What is behind is left there. So when she reaches a place of quiet the reflection is true and clear. There are no clouds carried from before."

He takes a small bundle from inside his shirt, opens it, and pulls out dried brown corn silks that have been twisted together at one end. He gently lays them in the front of the canoe, pointing the direction he will be going. He is bringing an element of earth to the journey—so the Mother of the Earth who breathes in the hair of the corn can guide his canoe as she guides life.

It had been a good crop this year and the guidance was strong. He knew it was time to answer the river's challenge, for she would be with him. He took the silk from the fifth row, from a sturdy stalk, and carried it through the winter, knowing when the first snows melted and the river swelled beyond herself, they would make the journey together.

Only one other time does he remember a crop so giving. He stood but eight harvests tall. His bones did not yet cast the shadow of strength and wisdom that the river demanded of a man alone in her waters. He helped his father prepare the canoe for the passage of many days. As he watched him disappear down the river his father's words echoed in the mist, "Someday you, too, will take the Mother of the Earth down the river. But you must wait for a good year to receive strong guidance."

Just as she soothes fear in the seed that becomes the plant—pushing through the earth to seek light, exposed to the elements—so, too, she will calm the fear within him as he faces the river and her challenge. As she protects the corn, she will protect him.

He cut the chosen tree and sang powerful songs of the river as he gave it shape. He knew the spirit of the tree would be strong. In his heart he asks if the vessel is worthy of his sacred companion.

He feels the answer, and smiles.

RIVER PLANT

As the water slides over rocks the river plant is lifted near the surface, roots burrowed deep in stones lining the stream bed, stem and leaves moving with the current.

The water twists and pulls, testing the will of the slender life. But without the river's dance, the plant could not stand. She would lie limp on the dry mud-covered stones.

She draws strength from the forces around her. The power that makes her dance can also uproot and fling her against the rocks.

THE FLOOD

D ays and nights of endless rain stretch behind him, turning the land into rivers of mud. He cannot see line where earth meets sky in any direction. The weight of the sky leaves him swollen and slow of breath. The sound as he walks through the forest has lost its crispness.

He remembers his father once telling him about a time of no sun, only rain, and how the earth did not grow right in that season. He explained to the young boy how at least once in a man's life he would know a season when things do not grow right. It is the test of days to salvage and rescue—to take very little and stretch to make it more. It is a time when every person's spirit is known.

His father remembered hunting lands along the river washed of the great trees. Boulders that only the Grandfathers could move rumbled thunder as the boiling water rolled them from their ancient places. He remembered the fear on his people's faces, the unasked question in their eyes—and always, the waiting for the sun.

Peaceful waters had become angry. A mighty will of strength and skill was needed to guide the canoe through places once familiar, now unknown. Destruction spread, yet despair did not follow. Determination led the way. The people did not stop... the rain did not stop... the people did not stop. Many fires were built each night to guide the moon upon her way, showing where they waited as she pulled the sleeping sun in her wake. Day and night, prayers were sung to wake the sun; to call the wind-who-dries-the-land.

Finally, the sky was empty and the earth knew rest. Ghost sun burning white through the grey began to draw the barreness and give her life again. She was painted with colors deep and clear.

Night skies pierced with points of light freed the moon to make her flight across the shadowed land. The healing had begun.

WATER FLOWERS

"Time brings about changes; some can be seen, some cannot. I remember a summer of my youth, lying on my belly by the pond. It was raining—slowly, quietly, no wind. The rain fell straight from the mouth of the sky. I was lying near a gathering of water flowers; pink and white, open to the sun. But they did not hold my heart. Instead, my eyes rested upon the leaf of the water flower: round, green, shiny, flat when I first looked, then not flat as I studied it; edges lifted, curled, bent, folded over, under, touching the water, out of the water.

"I liked the great ones in the rain. As I watched, a leaf would fill. I thought it would sink, but just as it became too full, a valley would appear and the water would run into the pond.

"The leaf would empty, fill again, another valley, and empty again.

"It was as if the one in the sky who gives rain was measuring the gift as each leaf slipped the offering into the clear water. Those changes took time, but I saw them happen. I did not see the pond rise."

MOON CHANGES

"The same moon that looks upon you looked upon me. She appears now as she did then. I wonder if we do.

"Sometimes in the passing of a night the world reveals itself to be a stranger. This we notice right away. Changes that happen with no movement or sound take us by surprise."

RUSTED NAIL

He holds a piece of time-bleached wood, fingers and thumb following pattern around a square, rusty nail—hands silently tracing his thoughts. He recalls leather thongs, stretched and tied, holding things together. He senses the nail is strong and full of promises that will push the leather into forgotten time. It marks his skin.

He decides he must carry it close to let it speak to him of days to come. Before sharing with the others in his camp he will ask the Old One for his wisdom.

Days spread around him, but still his insides remain clouded. The snows have come, and he buries the wood deep within a drift to let it sleep through the winter. He will not fill his head with questions. He asks the snow to listen to its secrets and when the land thaws, to reveal if this is something to be shared, or forgotten. As he places it under the snow, he removes it from his mind. He will not hold it again until spring.

BUFFALO

He stands on the crest of a hill overlooking a shallow valley. Buffalo rumblings drown all other sounds and cause the land to quake beneath his feet.

"It makes my heart glad to see my brothers free. To see them move as the wind—river of fur and dust rolling over the valley floor. I come here to be with them as they pass in spring—to see what tales they bring. Their fur speaks through thickness and color of winter's strength. Their numbers tell of buffaloes' strength. To watch them is to watch my people from a far place.

"The buffalo is noble and mighty. He takes nothing he cannot return. He asks nothing but water and a place to graze; not a costly creature for the earth to bear.

"Before the white man I never thought about the price demanded of the earth by those who walk her lands, but I do now. I did not know a creature lived that could take so much and give so little. Only a stranger to the earth could intrude this way—not a son of the earth.

"Maybe a bad seed landed upon the earth and she now suffers as its kind spread on the winds of sorrow. Hope lives in my heart that he will recognize the one who gives him life and will walk more gently.

"If he would run with the buffalo, not soak the bent grass with the smell of his brother's death, he could feel the connection. If he would listen to prairie grasses as they dance upon the earth he could hear the movement. If he would walk with the wind across the breast of the earth, he would know his roots.

"But he chooses to draw the death cloth across the face of all he touches. This I do not understand. I have never known a people who cast a shadow the sun could not touch.

"Running Wolf tells me he believes they come from a dark place of no sun. Their skin is pale, faces with no color, faces with no life; maybe faces with no soul. His words may explain how this can happen.

"The weight of a great sadness slows my breath."

HOUSE OF GLASS BOXES

I walked with you in the house where my people's things are kept behind glass. I looked with you and watched those around you. I had been there before.

"It is good to see things close to my heart, but the pain cuts like a knife dull from too many kills and no care.

"Some people look and try to understand. Others look and believe they understand. No one understands.

"The whites put the work of our hands in boxes of glass, nailed them to walls, arranged them according to their eye. It is a shadow of what they did to the people.

"When you look you see what they are. I see who they are. I hear them, smell them, touch them. A part of the spirit of each of us is in the glass boxes: the observed and the observer. When I look through the glass and see what is behind it, I also look more closely at the glass itself, and what is reflected in it. The images can be held separate, or they can be joined."

ASHES OF ANGER

The fire had snapped through the night, cooling to ash by morning. Faint trails of smoke rise from the charred wood scattered at his feet as he sits wrapped in heavy robes.

He dips the first two fingers of his right hand into the fine grey powder, then raises them to the sun. From deep inside him sounds come forth. He separates his fingers, the sun streams between, striking his forehead. He turns his hand around, fingers still parted, and draws a grey line on each side of the sun streak from hairline to browline.

His song builds as he presses the outside edge of his hand into the ashes. He sweeps it across his cheekbone to the side of his nose, down to the corner of his mouth and off his face.

Yesterday had been a day of anger. During the night, it was revealed to him that it would be wiser to wear his anger on his face, to be seen and known, than to keep it secret deep inside. He was told to cleanse his side-of-storm-clouds-gathering with the ashes of the day before.

He will wear the smudge of clouds through the day, and when fires burn this night he will walk to the river to wash his face clean again. The ashes of anger will be scattered by the water before they reach shore.

WISDOM OF THE TURTLE-SELF

He sits inside, the air damp and full. Listening to the rain beating on the skins of his teepee takes him to a place deeper than sun and wind can lead.

When the rain does not stop and the air cannot move he listens to the voices within that speak of things deep and quiet. He becomes more aware of his weight upon the earth; the weight of trees, horses, rocks.

The fire has not been lit in many days. Shadows swallow the lines of his face as he sinks into himself. Existence becomes a fine spider's thread suspended in air, leading nowhere. No sky above, no earth below; the weight of his bones hangs silent in midair.

Five days have passed since the sun gave warmth. The spirit of the camp lies still, waiting for the drumming on the skins to end. The children have stopped running in the water; excited voices and splashing no longer grace the air. They are inside and silent.

When no light comes from the sky, he looks to the small glowing place above his heart. It provides warmth. Other times of long rain he has built fires to dry and warm his lodge. This rain is a time of inner fires.

Two places breathe within him; the place of no movement, no warmth, no light, no sound; and the sister place that moves with warmth, light, and sound. He does not try to make them one, but keeps his awareness of both.

In the silent place he becomes stone that does not rest in earth or water—stone that floats in air. He sees inside himself, separated in the mist, islands that cannot touch. Here time hangs in a windless sky.

He sees, and knows what he must do to bring life into the places of stone. He has taken no food, no water, since the rain began. His vision is clear. Direction has been given; the final act before suspension dissolves and stone breathes.

He remembers a time of movement without guidance, sight without vision, sound without voice. He does not want this to happen again. He knows to hear the voice and not move would be a mockery and lay waste all that has been revealed.

So he leads his people in ways that allow the vision and the voice. A life of aimless motion becomes Earth that shrivels and dies: no shadow, no light; no silence, no sound—the place of void.

The rain stops as suddenly as it began. Slowly, wind begins to move his suspended self. A rhythm circles outward awakening the senses, ending the vision-dream.

The others wait for him to appear before they step into the fresh air. That night around the fire he will tell what he has seen and heard. They will know direction. They will mend the weak places. They will see new life where the poisons have been washed away.

He is an old man and has lived through the vision-rain before. Each time he has given thanks that the spirits found him worthy.

He has been the turtle inside its shell. Now he reaches out and touches the world. Those around the fire tonight will listen to his turtle-self and the wisdom from the spirit within the shell will speak.

SEABIRD

"I watched a seabird carry a mighty fish from the mouth of the water to the sky. Before its last breath the fish flew to heights only strong wings conquer.

"I dreamed that I might, with my final breath, soar the seabird's trail. It was the only gift I ever asked of the Great Spirit. I wanted to know what that fish knew."